The Way Through

The Way Through

Poems

Judith Kunst

Mayapple Press 2020

Published by   Mayapple Press
                 362 Chestnut Hill Road
                 Woodstock, NY 12498
                 mayapplepress.com

ISBN 978-1-936419-98-2
Library of Congress Control Number 2020937697

ACKNOWLEDGEMENTS

Grateful thanks to the editors of the following publications where these
poems, sometimes in different form or with different titles, first appeared:
*Able Muse, Broken Bridge Review, December, Image, Long Island Quarterly,
Measure, Poetry, Rock & Sling, Saint Katherine Review, Southern Poetry
Review,* and the Spark & Echo Arts Project.

Profound thanks also to these longtime readers and encouragers: Kevin
Kunst, Christine Perrin, Lavetta McCune, Sara Belk, Stevie Henry, Marie
Campbell, Susan Pilewski, Marlene Lee, Joy Sawyer, Jeannie Brennan,
Jessica Kantrowitz, Susi Leeming, Judy Oulund, Gina Bria, Paul Mariani,
Bill Shullenberger, Scott Cairns, Marie Howe, Suzanne Hoover, Elizabeth
Dishman, Glen McCune, Leslie Giles, and Aidan, Jesse, and Eli Kunst.

Cover art by Anita H. Lehman; author photo by Amanda Bultemeier. Book
design and layout by Judith Kerman, with text in Minion Pro and titles in
Book Antiqua.

Contents

Tenth Anniversary: Tin

I need you now
the way a window needs
a factory,

a float-glass facility
fitted out with huge furnaces
where sand can melt down

to liquid glass
and where something called
cassiterite can melt down

to liquid tin;
I need you now
the way hot glass needs

to pour itself out
on a shimmering surface,
a conveyer-belt river

of vitreous tin,
the one substance
on the planet that

won't cringe
when the hot glass hits
and spreads,

not mixing, not
adhering, glass spanning out
to an airy

thinness and cooling there,
floating, silvered
to a perfect smoothness.

This is the way I need you now,
when I get tired
the way a window must get

tired, holding itself
in the frame,
the way it must keep

thinking about that
factory: so much work
required to facilitate

such floating!
And such bright ease of un-
mingling almost

wholly inspired by what's
come after: the power
to see through walls.

I.

Long before glass,

I lay on a small square of bed in a small square of room
high in a building set in the triangle of Carmine & Bleeker
& Sixth. For one hot Manhattan summer I lay beneath
an open window which framed not sky but bricks, and
for ninety days I rode a train of moving squares to get to
a larger, unmoving square to stare at a square screen
that flickered, flickered.

That first night

I wandered Greenwich Village, too poor to step into
a restaurant or dance club, striking up random chats
in the street. Twice, three times, I spoke to a chauffeur who said
he was Oprah's favorite. I'd decided that only New Yorkers could be
writers, and I thought driving limos might allow me to be both and
also eat. I thought, *I'll write in the car while Oprah dances,* and
this part of the story always makes my husband laugh.

Prodigal Body

I walked into the Park and a man called out to me. He said,
Would you believe a year ago I weighed three hundred pounds?
I shook my head, and he said, *Nobody else will believe me either.*
His slender body showed at once the whole of his labor and
none: he was compelled to tell what had already been inscribed
in flesh. I wanted to say, *I too am a stranger to myself. I too have
taken to the streets.* But I'd not gained nor lost enough to speak.

In Idle Time Books on the twenty-second day,

already tiring of the fiction section, I bought my first book
of poems. I chose the thickest spine, the prettiest title,
Leaves of Grass, and by the time the subway spit me out
I was in love. Next day though, I was troubled. What kind of hero
doesn't think he needs to change? He called out *After me, vista!*
and I thought, *What an ego.* I hadn't learned how
to read him yet. How to read *us* for *me. You* for *vista.*

The Twenty-Ninth Day

Crossing Broadway at 81st suddenly my ankle turned
and I fell down in the street. Before I could move or
discover if I could move I felt hands gripping, lifting,
depositing me on the median bench between the traffic lights.
Oh, I exclaimed, turning to thank, to be further attended to
but my helper was gone, swallowed up by the city's
fervid rushy glittered yawn.

Reading Joseph Stroud

I wade in and immediately the force of the waves knocks me down
I wade in again and am again knocked down these waves of your
poems gobsmacking what I know your fierce curiosity, your curious
ferocity I wade in knock and blow I wade in break, shine, I look up
Cavafy Lorca Mandelstam Hawthorne Issa Rumi Stevens Yeats
Izumi Lu Yu Goya Celan revolving moons in your sky each one pulling
at the sea of your mind I wade in muscled song I wade in happy tide

My Date Lights a Cigarette Outside Carnegie Hall

Some part of my dad is still a young man, lying down
in the dark on some new bed in some new Texas town.
There's a radio propped on his chest; he's twirling its
plastic knob in search of Mozart or Schubert or Brahms.
Some part of my dad is still there listening, hard,
his lit cigarette just now finding the beat, a swinging
glowing path through static and the dark.

But After Three Great Dates He Left the City

I'll be in touch, he said, then carried his touch off to bricks
and sawn lumber, to boulders and bark, the steering wheel
of his truck, the head and the soft hair of someone else.
I went to St. Patrick's and knelt in the pew till I could say,
Touch them then. Touch your life. Don't think of me. Just
be in touch. And come away from nothing you have touched
unchanged.

Sunday Brunch on the Fifty-Third Day

On the Upper West Side, near her beloved Cloisters, in a kitchen
crammed with a two-foot statue of Shakespeare, a stuffed crow,
a hundred spice jars, my friend chops leeks for soup. She tells me
about her dream: how it felt to be grazed on, pierced by tree roots.
Then she laughs and refills our tiny wine glasses, which like me
seem grateful to be there. Later it will also seem natural to want,
like them, to pour what she's given me into other mouths.

On the Sixtieth Night I Dreamed I Was a *New Yorker* Cartoon

Inside the little outlined square I lie on my side, asleep and
modestly naked. Three pine trees grow on my shoulder, more
on my hip; two scribbled sheep stand chatting in the valley
of my waist. The sparse landscape must be part of the joke,
and I can feel myself smiling—but I can't see the caption
floating under the frame. My knees, feet, and most of my
head are also outside it. In here, I am nothing but ground.

Leaves of Grass: **The Musical**

How Whitman would have loved that dream! He loved
lying naked on the ground. Yet not for him any long
slumber, any holding still for fear of toppling the sheep.
Not for him any long pondering of borders nor of captioning
his life or any life. Oh look now yes he is sitting up, gathering
lambs & shaggy trees in his arms, he has busted the frame,
he is breaking into song.

Looking for Easier Ways to Say *"New Yorker* Cartoon Dream"

Are all icons such heavy suitcases, carrying so much
that's essential inside them? Clearly well-designed
yet so awkward to lug around, containing for you
what you couldn't begin to contain for yourself?
Guaranteeing that while you're away from home you'll
have everything you need, but that always the world
will look, to you and at you, a little bit skewed?

The Caption Speaks

I don't mind being set off like this, apart from the madding crowds,
the endless word streams marching in their fixed columns. I don't mind
the solitude—it seems a fair exchange for that moment of almost
laughter, that grunt of comprehension as the reader turns the page.
I do wish you could see what I say. You're at the heart of this thing!
I'd love to call myself out to you, present you the joke. But I don't have
a voice, you understand. I am the summing up.

On the Eighty-Third Day a Dear Friend Gives Birth

Welcome to the circus! Soon enough we'll give you cream pies to fill,
a red nose to wear. You'll climb rafters, clap when your dad dances
with lions. None of us will say *wait till you're older*—for the weather
will get colder. We'll lower the long poles, fold up the tents, hoist
the magic carpets on our shoulders. You'll walk in front, between the
elephants, where you can see the new road winding down. You'll privately
practice your *Ladies and gents!* while I plaster the ads in the next town.

The Midwife

She is not the wife of the intellectual. Not the wife of the woodsman.
Not the wife of the architect, or the Zambian student, or the folksinger,
ex-priest, or Marine. She knows a hundred different smiles.
Grows arms to hold the widower and weeps to see him sleep.
Learns new words: dyslexia, kwaheri, theodicy, clearcut. Navigates
highways and rivers and fear, kills pity, hammers on God's chest.
Let the wife say *I love you*. She says *I love*.

Reading Anselm Kiefer

I'd never have guessed, walking into St. Mark's Bookshop after that
dismal party in the East Village, how happily my troubled virgin poems
would begin to be resolved by an artist in Barjac, France, who for years
had painted himself lying nude beneath the night sky, who'd layered clay &
darkness & light on canvas, aiming not so much to sell the glossy book I'd
carry home that night as to render on paper the sky that presses,
the swerve of planet that lifts & possesses.

On the hottest day of that hot summer

I remembered shadows crossing cement, harsh cries arrowing
over my head, the soccer field next to our house taken
by wild geese, trampling and shitting each morning for months
in the winter. I remembered climbing the chain link fence to sit
in the spattered white field. I remembered saying out loud
I want this—the broad sky glowing on the mountains and houses,
the feather marks brushed in the snow.

Crying was heard behind the brick wall,

but it was not like the crying of children, for nothing in it remotely resembled innocence. It was not like the crying of boiled water in a kettle, for water does not start a fire under itself, nor does water keep boiling when its kettle has been crushed. If only the crying had been like that of wild geese: then I could've heard in those sobs some hope of pattern, some syncopation of departure and return. There was not. Any.
And for once comparisons would not console.

Reading Simone Weil

Beauty is a fruit we look at without
trying to seize it. If Weil is right, there is no
beauty in New York. On the seventieth day
I saw a walking priest, his pace exquisitely
slow. His purpose, I decided, was to make time
beautiful again. But this was in a movie.
And just the one scene.

Fourth Floor Escape

The iron ladders let me climb them. The small grated cell
let me sit in brown dust at what seemed a heavenly height.
I could almost touch the tops of lindens, tall & thin
& throbbing like a choir. I could almost believe the saint's
words—*You cannot wander anywhere that will not
aid you*—and by believing mean accept: no place exists
that will let me keep pretending I'm not lost.

Closed Door

Time & Money have loved this city longest and they
will not share. It is the ninetieth day. I follow the sign, Request
Rare Books, to a room as large and quiet as a church
and ask to hold Weil's essay one more time. New York light
touches the words in my lap. I lay my hands on them too.
This world is the closed door, they say. *And at the same time
it is the way through.*

II.

I-80 West at Sunset

Into the rushing dark
   a hundred starlings rise,
a hundred breaths, two hundred,
   oh a thousand climb
the air, their single body
   swelling like a lung inhaling sky and
still more sky, wings lifted into light
   already fallen as they turn
& dive to girder nests beneath the highway.

I'm hushed in my fast car, just
   passing the bridge when they're
up again, wavering now in the dusk
      like a broad and casual hand,
         raised for a moment then dropped—
            and I'm reeling,
         swept to the edge
      of the highway and left

               with what but to follow
                  on foot.

LaPorte, Indiana

The land here is unexpectedly hilly, as if
the Great Plains had hunched up in surprise
at running into an equally Great Lake,

as if God, sitting on his tailor's stool, had plucked
at a long thread of river and pulled.

Or as if, watching the very first humans arrive,
the land had raised its foresty eyebrows,
wrinkling its face into a permanent

state of expectation.

Genesis

The night we married, making love,
my husband nudged my left hip loose.
He lay beside me like a god. I thought,
I will not let you go until you bless me.

Funny, not until love felled me did I fall
in love, my body opened wide, my coiled
mind set loose to seize on the ancient story:
Jacob limping, wounded, hip dislodged...

Here was a man who knew love
when he saw it, who clutched the loose
threads of heaven and hauled, all thought
tensed toward demand: *Bless me.*

And God blessed him, tied his loose
life tight to a new name, *One Who Strives with God
and Lives.* And Jacob slept. But I, until
this long dream ends, lie stumped in thought.

He is no god who set me limping.
How does a wounded love love?
Here in the dark love's been set loose,
been sealed; and God holds his own thoughts

till we awaken, limping, healed.

At Sea

You are sleeping now and I am folding your itty-bitty laundry,
tiny garments that slide through my hands like little fish
with silvery snaps for eyes. Some have funny
stiff collars attached, which on a fish might serve
for navigation or propulsion, but on you?

Years ago I stood on a dock and watched the waves
come billowing toward me. I thought, *Far away,*
God is shaking out the bedclothes.

Now you are sleeping in your crib and
I am the god, and my great
clumsy hands cannot fold these little shirts
nor keep them from swimming away.

Third Anniversary: Leather

As to the hide, how long
till scrapers can be
set aside and polish cloths
and brushes taken up?

As to stitching, how much
hemp, how many holes
will keep the soft skin fastened
to the sole's persistent rocking?

Such questions are moot, or rather,
mute: if the foot's learned anything
by now, it knows it cannot tame
the boot by talking.

Two Ways

Some people can surf
a whole sea of secrets.
Tossed on waves of
innocent inquiries
or sucked toward
riptides of the seriously
curious, their sun-
kissed, shut-lipped,
upright ease achieves
silence's buoyancy.

Others can't surf—
can't even swim.
They have to build
a secrets museum.
What shouldn't be told
gets framed out in gold
& carefully lit, best
displaying for viewers
who won't be admitted
vivid confessions
that won't be exhibited.

Choking Hazard

When you were two I swept the kitchen,
keeping you safe from dead bugs, odd
pennies, Legos, gum, and a tiny yellow ball
I only dimly perceived was being

grabbed and put back,
day after day grubby-grabbed from the trash
and put back in the dusty corner precisely
where you wanted it.

Way back then I was amused, delighted,
called it your *ardor for order*.
Now you are older and oh I see:
it was danger you couldn't live without.

Reading Emily Dickinson

Work, says
the right hand.
Love, says the left.
Down below,
the muddy rooted heart
says *lark* and *wove* and
crewel and *whorl.*
Says *whelk, evoke*—she's
loving this—
Velcro!
                    No,
say the hands,
and sigh, and try again.

Accept, says the left.
Achieve, says the right.
Gesundheit! says the heart.

But When They Came Home I Chose the Lesser Joy

Every morning for a week while the children were at school
I walked through our new woods. One day I found five old
tires hanging from wires tied way up in the trees. Five
floating portals. Monster pentoculars. A rowdy crowd
of zeros. I thought of the children's joy when I announced
this discovery—and of their greater joy should I keep silent,
let them find it for themselves—

Album

There's the one with my dad and his cigarette.
Then there's the one where he
leans in toward the woodwinds, listens,
nods, and with a tender gesture calls
legato from the strings.

And oh here's the one where
the nervous soprano
started her solo
four beats too late

and Dad with his two bare hands
—Paul Bunyan in a tux,
Moses with a much smaller staff—
grabbed that orchestra's
Mississippi of sound and
rerouted it.

At the Lake

We walk to the end of the dock and lie down on our bellies.
He says, *The water looks green,* and stirs it with his stick.

I say, *Look, you're cleaning the dirt off that stick,* and he says,
That's not dirt, that's tiny dancers. I say *Oh,* and he says,

On the stick they just dance slower. After a while he says, *Let's go,*
so we push ourselves up to walk over the sand. He says,

Here is a feather for you, bend down, and he tucks it behind
my ear. He says, *Do you want this piece of rock?* and

I want to say, *How will it fit behind my ear?* but the sand
and the wind and the lake say, *Listen,* so I hold out my hand

and he says, *This is a piece of the world,* and closes my
fingers over the rock, and together we walk to the car.

Consolation

I know it isn't easy being you.
Your friend has run crying
to tell his father that you've
hit him with a rock

& you've told me, yourself
crying, that you did it but don't
know why. Pity has come up in my
throat & swelled out

between us, a delicate thing
that both of us see and one of us
dimly understands. When at last
it's time for bed, I know you will ask

to have the covers pulled up
and to have me rub you all over,
pressing you into sleep
or into yourself,

brushing off the day or sealing
it in—whatever metaphor
will relieve us & keep us
for the time being.

(In) Sufficient

Not much was harder than saying out loud *You're right,*
we got it wrong. But in out-louding the *wrong,* we were also saying
You're right and *We got it.* And though you insisted that we'll
never get *it*—and there are signs to suggest *you're right*—
still, that day, we *got,* somewhere, somehow, trying
to *right* our *wrong.* A little bit closer to *You are,* maybe.
A little bit closer to *we.*

(In) Sufficient

I said, *Sorry I lost my temper back there.*
You said, *No problem, I understand.*

I said, *How could I have so easily lost my there?*
You said, *My no stands under your there; it cannot be lost.*

I said, *My temper is a sorry thing.*
You said, *Your sorry is a hammer, tempering you with
many delicate blows into a thing of strength & beauty.*

I said, *Will you be the table on which this thing can rest?*
You said, *Yes.*

For the Work

Four thick wires tangle in your hands, caught
and snaking like a busted gyroscope.
You know you should have given this more thought.

Bend, loop and thread each strand to form a knot
and then a path of knots. Stay loose and grope
along; hope your hand, tangling, won't get caught.

Do some lucky people get to be taught
this awkward art? Learn the work and its scope
beforehand, know how to give it more thought?

It's time; you think, *I'll only get one shot
to pull this off.* You're filled with faith and hope,
thick wires finely tangled, finally caught:

There! Do you love its beauty, now it's taut?
Yes, if beauty's wrestling, if love is rope.
(You know you could be giving this more thought.)

Work too much talked about is overwrought.
You've made a necklace, not a stethoscope.
Four wires tangled in your hands were caught.
Perhaps you needn't give it much more thought.

Reading Francis Thompson

Dreaming again, this time in a house
high on a seaside cliff. I wander out to see
a laundry line stretched across the courtyard,
hung with a pair of enormous black wings.

The scene shifts to my own plain home.
I'm showing my husband a poem which,
though I've written it, ends with a word I do not
recognize, even when I wake: *Intercease*.

Mutual stopping? Communal rest?
Search for it, like I did, online. Find it,
like I did, only in his poems.

(I don't enjoy reading them. They are
heavy, smothering, difficult to lift
and pin.)

Reading Abraham Joshua Heschel

Not in the least embarrassed to be seen
through the window of the kitchen where
I'm washing dinner dishes and yelling
to my son about a pencil sharpener,
the sky drapes her delicate pink undergarments
over the trees, the clouds, the neighbor's house.
Heschel said, *Faith is a blush in the presence
of God.* And I see that the sky isn't
unembarrassed, but profoundly shy.
And I see that she continues to undress.
And that I continue to look.

Dancing with Orion

At twelve you see so little and so much
in seven stars: two hands and feet, a belt,
a man. To find him takes all terror out of night
though sometimes, unaccountably, you weep
beneath his gaze. At Halloween, you string
electric lights around your arms and twirl:
a wild star-dancer loosed upon the world.
You've not yet learned your archer friend
will climb down laddered months and disappear.
Oh my son, will you ever again look up
in hope or trust at the glorious dark?
Ever again go outside, lie down in the grass
and feel the earth's curve, the heavy dance
that offers you so little and so much?

Found Horizon

Here, at the *apparent junction of earth and sky,*
tangent to earth's surface at one observer's

position with the celestial sphere,
my husband sleeps.

The curve of his cheek on the pillow
and the rising light behind that

stubborn stubble represent
something that might be attained.

And the husk of anger I've hugged to myself all night
loosens and falls away.

Though not without effort, for the line
laid out across this

range of experience or perception
stretches from deed to thoughtless deed

like a wire fence I have to stoop beneath
to sidle past.

The consequent curve in my spine
just meets his body's broad line.

Then even that
reasonably distinct boundary
recedes.

III.

The Crow

Was it because
at last
I cleaned the window

that he threw himself
against the glass?
I thought, poor crow—

he doesn't know
the evergreens
and blue sky

are behind him.
I turned back
to my page

but *whumpp*—
the bird attacked
the glass again.

His long claws
scuffled at the pane
and I yelled, "Crow!

Go away!"
Again his body
slapped the glass,

again,
and then again,
and then at last

he caught my eye—
oh, prophet,
terrified.

Our Lady of the *New Yorker* Cartoon

Like a broad and casual hand, raised for a moment
then dropped: disaster struck my friend. One day chopping leeks
in a kitchen stuffed with spice jars, and the next:

Like all the rest of us she can't stop thinking
about her body: how it fell: how it broke: fell and spilled
and broke in a way that keeps her alive and horribly:

*

My Indiana life goes on, crowded and important to me
but far from the bed framed in my phone where she lies
on her side, unmoving and modestly naked:

over the noise of TV she can't shut off she tells me:
Parkinson's meds work better with coffee the hospital
won't serve. Paralysis doesn't mean you can't feel when

you're being touched, and the loneliness of underpaid aides
is perilous. Christian to her now means: one who notices
you need to wipe your nose and wipes your nose.

*

Finally I visit, bring coffee, poems. When she falls asleep,
I lipstick an X on her window glass and go outside: find
my mark to know her room: push past shrubs & pine trees

to hunker down where hospital brick and earth meet.
I'm not hiding. Not praying. I'm looking for the caption
that must lie beneath:

Reading Walt Whitman

Head, neck, hair, ears,
tongue, lips, teeth,

> Sometimes we see a person and immediately
> reject them, as a person and even

roof of the mouth, throat
the lung-sponges, the stomach-sac,

> as an animate object.
> They are to us nothing more than

the ample side-round of the chest,
O I say these are not

> neon rubber traffic cones
> to be avoided.

the parts and poems
of the body only

> Yet without such bright mute shouting guides,
> what tragedies might befall

but of the soul. O my body!
I dare not desert the likes of you!

> we who rush
> from competence to competence?

The Caption Speaks

Let me be still.
Let breathing slow in me.
Let me throw off light, and shed water.
Let me rest between upheavals let me rest.
Let me hold the dark spaces. Let me cave.
Let me be heft in the hand, flint chip and spark.
Let chisel. Let mallet. Let ax.
Let all gleam in my veins be cut to bedrock.
Let me be. Let me be.
Axis to the earth's deep whirling.

Reading the Bible

Snap the ropes off your arms as if
they were threads. Stumble at midday as if
it were twilight. Grope through the streets as if
you were blind. Go into the inner part of the house as if
to get some wheat. Remember those in prison as if
you were with them in prison. Clothe yourself
from the waist up with glowing metal, as if
brilliant light surrounds you, as if
you were going farther, as if
you were filled with fire.

In the middle of the woods I take off my shoes

and my world's
weirdly contracted,
also huge:
like walking
through a house
that's blown a fuse,
my feet
slow feelers
touching, oh—
something sharp:
the memory
of your face.
My blundering
search through
years, through
every street.
My thinking
I saw you once
& touching
your arm.
The stranger
saying *no honey,*
I'm sorry.
And then
the walking home,
my heart con-
tracted, huge.
A dark house.
A blown fuse.

Haystacks

Teach me. What else is there to ask these
stacks of paint and light, these lit humps
of wheat on broad fields pulling me through
the framed wall?

Monet was the first to see that color hides
inside a shifting crowd of
weather, time, shadow, shape,
the structure of our eyes.
He was the first to build an easel
he could take outside to paint,
looking, and look, painting,
until he'd proved it. Or caught it.
Or freed it.

And suddenly a man calls out to me.
You dropped your pen. By the far stairs?
At the end of the Modern Wing.
We are standing among haystacks
and hundreds of people.
I think about my graying
hair, my bright green sweater:
remembered and watched for.

There is gold in the sky. There is pink
on the ground. The stacks are crimson
or teal or browny-gray, depending
on Claude's eyes, my eyes,
the time of day. The face of the man
who sought me out is turning a silvery blue.
He tilts his head. *Might still be there,* he says.
And when I go looking, it is.

Reading Vassar Miller

Against the stone wall a maple
is shaking her hair out,
pulling her fingers through
lanky red locks
spilling over her shoulders,
her corseted chest,
each siren leaf laughing,
not afraid to be gorgeous,
not afraid to say yes
to the long brittle fall.

Never famous. Never rich.
Never mother. Never wife.
Never anything at all
outside the singing
of her books.
Never anything but faithful
to the singing she heard
singing, to the labor
of the listening
which became the living singing
of her books.

The Ink Speaks to the Page

Everything in me wants to touch you.
I am besotted by your silence and by
watching myself break it.

Nothing for me
outside the boundaries of your clean white frame
holds meaning.

Yes the internet and its efficiency.
Yes ecology. But surely zeroes
cannot feel about ones

the way I feel about you,
the way touching you calls forth from me
a permanence.

Prodigal Body

Once while I was walking, a man called out to me.
He was slender, sitting on the grass with a racing
bike beside him. He said, *Would you believe a year ago*

I weighed three hundred pounds? I shook my head,
and he said, *Nobody else will believe me either.*
His body showed at once the whole of his labors

and none. He was compelled to tell
what had already been inscribed in flesh,
to repeatedly salute not what he once was

nor what he'd become but the fact, the choice,
the very moment and infinite moments
of change itself. Could no one return

this salute? What if he'd gotten up off the grass,
stepped out on the path and touched me
on the shoulder? What if we'd said vows,

shed clothing, faced each other in the dark—
could I have believed him then? Would he
have believed my believing?

Reading Simone Weil

Beauty is a fruit we look at
without trying to seize it.

My hurt friend longs for a pen. Paper.
She is composing all the time in her head.

We used to consider the good poem
a seized thing, a frame for beauty.

Now? *The fruit of not*
seizing is beauty.

The trying and failing to seize
is beauty.

If one's beauty has been seized—has seized—
can it still bear fruit?

If one is relieved
of the ability to seize beauty,

is one also relieved
of the ability to destroy it?

I'm a quaddy, my friend says,
not a saint.

The Ink Speaks of My Friend

Like a bird perched at the top of a swaying tree, her bed
tilts and swerves as the planet tilts and swerves. She is being,
moved—and like the planchette of wood on a Ouija board,
like the barrel of a pen gripped by a fist, her bed spells out
astonishing songs. (I know readers will challenge me on this.
Like her, they will say, I lack agency. Like her
I am every day more and more spilled out.)

(In) Sufficient

The geometry of sunslant
blocks my earthbound angle,
and I can't ID the bird
weightlessly perched, songsmithing
in the pine tree by my house.
The sun & I stare and stare till I see:
the tree is dying.

                    I'm afraid,
I said to the professor: *if the ending*
isn't happy, then the story isn't true.
The bird I want to catalog
keeps singing. The tree and the sun
sway and sway.

My professor said *In this life*
you may insist on neither happy
nor true, *nor* story, *nor even*
ending. *Only* if *and* the,
she said. *Only* isn't *and* then.

Fifteenth Anniversary: Crystal

When the poet said,
Even between the closest people
infinite distances exist,

x-ray crystallography
had yet to be discovered.
Nobody knew

how perfectly the spaces
between latticed atoms
in a crystal—salt, agate,

diamond—would fit
the waves of an x-ray beam,
or with what precision that beam,

shining through those spaces,
would map our path
to powerful new places.

All these years
I've been giving you
simile after simile,

shoehorning leather and tin
and the like into love poems;
all these years we've been

testing hypotheses about
happiness and time and
togetherness and now,

as I push words like
elastic scattering and
constructive interference

over the latticed page,
I marvel once more
that refracted seeing

can be trusted, that
everywhere we look for love,
we find love.

Acknowledgements

My thanks to the silver beech I passed every day
on my walk to work; to the poolside slab of hot concrete
I lay down on as a child; to the white curtain that waved
in the windows of all my houses; to the small boy in the car
who said *I need a medicine called Never Mind*;
and to the constellation Orion, who championed me
and pushed me beyond where I thought I could go.

Notes

"Fifth Anniversary: Crystal": Quoted lines are taken from Rainer Maria Rilke, *Letters to a Young Poet*.

"Found Horizon": Quoted lines are taken from Webster's Dictionary definition of "horizon."

"Fourth Floor Escape": Quoted line has been attributed variously to St. Francis and to Rabi'a al-Basri.

"Haystacks": The paintings referred to are "Stacks of Wheat" in the Art Institute of Chicago.

"Reading Abraham Heschel": Quoted line is taken from Heschel's *I Asked for Wonder: A Spiritual Anthology*.

"Reading Anselm Kiefer": See in particular Kiefer's painting "The Renowned Orders of the Night," which you can find here: *https://www.guggenheim-bilbao.eus/en/the-collection/works/the-renowned-orders-of-the-night*.

"Reading the Bible": Quoted lines are taken from my study of the phrase "as if" as it occurs in English translations of the Bible.

"Reading Joseph Stroud" and "But When They Came Home…": These poems and the whole of Part I are deeply indebted to Stroud's "A Suite for the Common" in *Below Cold Mountain*.

"Reading Simone Weil": Quoted lines are taken from Weil's *Gravity and Grace*. The essay in "The Closed Door" is the 1939 edition of *Les Cahiers du Sud* in which Weil's "The Iliad or The Poem of Force" first appeared.

"Reading Walt Whitman": Quoted lines are taken from "I Sing the Body Electric" in *Leaves of Grass*.

About the Author

Poems by Judith Kunst have appeared in *Poetry, December, Image, Able Muse, Measure, Southern Poetry Review, Saint Katherine Review, In Posse,* and, as Judith McCune, in *The Atlantic.* Paraclete Press published her first book *The Burning Word: A Christian Encounter with Jewish Midrash* in 2006. She makes her home with her husband and three sons in Evansville, Indiana, where she works as a grant writer for Youth First, Inc.

Other Recent Titles from Mayapple Press:

Ellen Stone, *What Is in the Blood*, 2020
      Paper, 72pp, $17.95 plus s&h
      ISBN 978-1-936419-95-1
Terry Blackhawk, *One Less River*, 2019
      Paper, 78pp, $16.95 plus s&h
      ISBN 978-1-936419-89-0
Ellen Cole, *Notes from the Dry Country*, 2019
      Paper, 88pp, $16.95 plus s&h
      ISBN 978-1-936419-87-6
Monica Wendel, *English Kills and other poems*
      Paper, 70pp, $15.95 plus s&h
      ISBN 978-1-936419-84-5
Charles Rafferty, *Something an Atheist Might Bring Up at a Cocktail Party*, 2018
      Paper, 40pp, $14.95 plus s&h
      ISBN 978-1-936419-83-8
David Lunde, *Absolute Zero*, 2018
      Paper, 82pp, $16.95 plus s&h
      ISBN 978-1-936419-80-7
Jan Minich, *Wild Roses*, 2017
      Paper, 100pp, $16.95 plus s&h
      ISBN 978-1-936419-77-7
John Palen, *Distant Music*, 2017
      Paper, 74pp, $15.95 plus s&h
      ISBN 978-1-936419-74-6
Eleanor Lerman, *The Stargazer's Embassy*, 2017
      Paper, 310pp, $18.95 plus s&h
      ISBN 978-936419-73-9
Dicko King, *Bird Years*, 2017
      Paper, 80pp, $14.95 plus s&h
      ISBN 978-936419-69-2
Eugenia Toledo, tr. Carolyne Wright, *Map Traces, Blood Traces /*
      Trazas de Mapas, Trazas de Sangre, 2017
      Paper, 138pp, $16.95 plus s&h
      ISBN 978-936419-60-9
Eric Torgersen, *In Which We See Our Selves: American Ghazals*, 2017
      Paper, 44pp, $14.95 plus s&h
      ISBN 978-936419-72-2

For a complete catalog of Mayapple Press publications, please visit our website at *www.mayapplepress.com*. Books can be ordered direct from our website with secure on-line payment using PayPal, or by mail (check or money order). Or order through your local bookseller.